# ABSTRACT ART

# PATTERNS AND DESIGNS

Ad. AND M. P. VERNEUIL

INTRODUCTION BY

## Steven Calloway

ASSISTANT CURATOR OF PAINTINGS
VICTORIA AND ALBERT MUSEUM,
LONDON

BRACKEN BOOKS
LONDON

PUBLISHED BY BRACKEN BOOKS
A DIVISION OF BESTSELLER PUBLICATIONS LTD
PRINCESS HOUSE, 50 EASTCASTLE STREET
LONDON W1N 7AP
ENGLAND

*ABSTRACT ART PATTERNS AND DESIGNS*
IS A SELECTION OF PLATES FROM
*KALEIDOSCOPE*
*ORNEMENTS ABSTRAITS*
BY AD. AND M. P. VERNEUIL
ÉDITIONS ALBERT LEVY
2, RUE DE L'ÉCHELLE
PARIS
1925

THE PLATES IN THIS VOLUME HAVE BEEN REPRODUCED
DIRECTLY FROM *KALEIDOSCOPE*. ANY IMPERFECTIONS
ARE DUE TO THE AGE AND QUALITY OF THE ORIGINALS.
THE READER SHOULD REGARD THESE FACSIMILE
REPRODUCTIONS AS FAITHFUL TO THE PRESENT CONDITION
OF THE VERNEUILS' WORK.

POSTER ART SERIES

*ABSTRACT ART PATTERNS AND DESIGNS*
IS A VOLUME IN THE BRACKEN POSTER ART
SERIES. UP TO TEN PLATES MAY BE
REPRODUCED IN ANY ONE PROJECT OR
PUBLICATION, WITHOUT SPECIAL PERMISSION
AND FREE OF CHARGE. WHEREVER POSSIBLE THE
AUTHOR, TITLE AND PUBLISHER SHOULD BE ACKNOWLEDGED
IN A CREDIT NOTE. FOR PERMISSION TO MAKE MORE EXTENSIVE USE
OF THE PLATES IN THIS BOOK APPLICATION
MUST BE MADE TO THE PUBLISHER.

ISBN 1 85170 152 4

PRINTED IN ITALY

# INTRODUCTION

The fine series of decorative books by the Verneuils, Adam and the, now, better remembered Maurice, forms a highly important link between the work of the great ornamentists of the middle and later years of the nineteenth century and that extraordinary outburst of design talent in the Paris of the twenties; a link between the confidently eclectic tastes of the nineteenth century style manuals and the bold manifestoes of avant-garde design. In the world of decoration and the applied arts that new spirit found its greatest expression in the celebrated *Exposition des Arts Décoratifs* in 1925. The strengths and indeed the weaknesses of that show have become the touchstones by which we measure the achievements of the host of decorative artists, furniture makers and pattern designers, both French and of other nations, who worked in the exciting and colourful modernistic style which dominated the commercial design world in the inter-war years, and from the name of the show itself we derive that useful, if sometimes rather vaguely applied style-name, *Art Deco*.

On turning the vibrantly coloured pages of *Kaleidoscope* (published 1925), the book of 'ornements abstraits' from which the present selection of plates has been drawn, it seems so much to be the epitome of a new and youthfully exuberant style that it comes as something of a shock when we realize the position it occupies, not at the beginning of a young designer's career, but rather as the culmination for the Verneuils of more than a quarter of a century of aesthetic exploration and technical innovation in the production of books of decorative design.

Maurice Pillard Verneuil was born in 1869 in St. Quentin in the Aisne, and his early development seems very typical of a whole generation of late-nineteenth century artists and designers whose talents were first directed by earnest provincial teachers along the well-trodden paths of the French academic tradition. The teaching system of the day, in France as in England and Germany, laid the greatest importance on the acquisition of proficiency and correctness in drawing, which was in itself an admirable ideal and one which tended to give students a firm foundation of practical skill. However the system also tended to perpetuate an antiquated scale of relative values which placed at the very pinnacle of achievement drawing of the human figure from life, for this was seen as the proper preparation for the highest calling in art: the painting of figure subjects on literary, historical or religious themes. Other branches of drawing, such as designing for the manufacture of objects or the creation of flat pattern for textiles and wallpapers, were accorded only lowly stations in this scheme of artistic endeavour.

With the gradual freeing of painting from the domination of the academic tradition in the latter part of the nineteenth century, some of the more rigid distinctions between fine and applied art began increasingly to become blurred. Collaborations between painters, architects and craftsmen led to a greater interchange of skills and the status of the designer began to rise. In England the example and teachings of William Morris did much to encourage the concept of the interrelationship of all the arts and his writings, along with the books of Dr. Christopher Dresser and Owen Jones, placed pattern design on an entirely new footing. At the South Kensington Schools, the fountainhead of all art teaching in England, pattern design began to be systematically taught, whilst a steady stream of books published in England and in France attests to the increasingly widespread and serious interest in the subject.

In France where the great encyclopedic pattern books of historic style by Lacroix and Viollet-le-Duc were distinguished principally by their painstaking scholarship, we can observe the emergence of a new kind of publication in which the concerns of colour and texture and the purely formal values of pattern making begin to dominate. Eugène Grasset (1845–1917) was the crucial figure in the development of these exciting new graphic forms and his work, strongly influenced by the flat colour and stylized drawing of Japanese printmaking rapidly became widely admired and imitated. The adoption of highly stylized plant forms, and in particular of the whiplash tendril motif, as a basis for the design both of flat pattern and for objects to be made in metal, ceramic or glass became a cornerstone of the whole *Art Nouveau* movement and few young and emergent designers at this period were untouched by the influence.

Grasset's own 'school' of pupils and assistants were naturally encouraged, true to the traditions of the French *atelier* system, to work in their master's style, and several of the most promising including Maurice Pillard Verneuil and the young Augusto Giacometti (brother of the famous sculptor) were entrusted with the preparation of the exquisite coloured plates for Grasset's great volumes, *La Plante et ses Applications Ornementales* of 1897. For Verneuil the project was a revelation and a turning point, introducing him both to the stylistic path which his work would take and to the *pochoir* process, the technical means by which he would realise his own remarkable series of design books.

In essence the *pochoir* printing process is very simple and involves the use of stencils to produce areas of flat colour laid over an outline from a printed key-plate, or merely built up one upon the next to form an arrangement of pure colour. In practice of course the method is highly complex and, in the hands of a good designer who is served by skilled craftsmen, capable of the most extraordinary richness and delicacy of effect. Verneuil's first independent production was a volume based on Grasset's *La Plante* and devoted to the adaptation of the forms of animals to the purposes of decoration, but his next venture was a work devoted to extolling the possibilities of the medium itself, *l'Ornementation par le Pochoir*, which appeared in 1898.

By this date Verneuil was establishing a reputation as a decorative artist and had begun to design posters which appeared on the Paris hoardings alongside the more celebrated productions of Jules Chéret and Toulouse-Lautrec. Although his designs never reached the level attained by those masters of the art, some of his work for *Le Monde Moderne* and *Le Laurenol* is remembered and his design for *Docteur Pierre's Toothpaste* is still sometimes reproduced in books on poster design.

In 1901 Verneuil collaborated with the two major figures, Alphonse Mucha and Georges Auriol in an intriguing volume of designs, which in some ways pre-figures the present collection in its use of an optical conceit in the production of a pattern book, *Combinaisons Ornementales se multipliant à l'Infini à l'aide du Miroir*. The succeeding years saw a constant stream of works on the application of various natural forms to decorative design: insects in 1904 followed by fish in 1905, reptiles the next year and birds in 1907. By 1908 Verneuil's interests had again turned to the technical processes of reproducing colour images and he published in that year *Le Procédé de Gravure en trois Couleurs*.

By the end of the decade the *Art Nouveau* style in decoration was distinctly on the wane and Verneuil's interests seem to have moved increasingly towards the arts of the East. His work on Japanese textiles was published in London in 1910 and these oriental researches eventually led, after many years, to the publication of his pioneering study, *l'Art à Java*, in 1927. It may well be that Verneuil first became seriously fascinated in abstract or 'pure' pattern-making in this way rather than through more direct contact with Parisian avant-garde painters and designers who were feeling their way towards abstraction and colour-based art at this time. The years immediately before and after the Great War saw in Paris an extraordinary degree of experimentation and the relatively rapid forging of an entire new artistic vocabulary, which quickly spread from the fine arts of painting and sculpture to influence decoration. Indeed one of the most fascinating aspects of the emergence of the new movements: Cubism, Vorticism, Fauvism and many others, is the way in which they were so rapidly assimilated as stylistic influences into the work of the more aware and receptive designers and decorators.

Even before the war in England, Roger Fry and his Bloomsbury artist friends were, in their rather haphazardly run Omega Workshops, producing artefacts and painted decoration which owed an obvious allegiance to the Parisian post-Impressionist avant-garde. Not just in painting, but in decoration and in fashion, flat, abstracted pattern ruled the day and, under the influence of Diaghilev's Russian Ballet which shot like an exotic meteor across Europe, extravagant and vibrant colour coruscated on walls and floors, on furniture and in women's dresses; reaching a heady crescendo in about 1919. Bold geometric forms, some amply rounded and some aggressively angular, but all recalling the barbaric splendours of African tribal textiles became the rage in Paris, whilst the painters, such as Robert Delaunay, whose canvases were beautifully crafted exercises in colour, found their work imitated in upholstery fabric and in the very carpets beneath their feet.

It was in this milieu, which culminated in the splendours of the *Art Deco* style at the Paris exhibition of 1925 that Maurice Pillard Verneuil, by this time well into middle-age, abandoned the sombre colour schemes of his earlier years, those sage greens and purples of *Art Nouveau*, and, taking up the brilliant palette of the young, utilized the *pochoir* process, of which he remained an almost unsurpassed master, to create *Kaleidoscope*, his great swan-song and one of the acknowledged masterpieces of the *Deco* style.

STEPHEN CALLOWAY
ASSISTANT CURATOR OF PAINTINGS
VICTORIA AND ALBERT MUSEUM
NOVEMBER 1987

# THE POSTER ART SERIES

## THE PLATES

PLATE 2

Left: *Non-repeating border design of asymmetrical shapes in reds and purples. (Detail of* plate 1)

Right: *Non-repeating border design of asymmetrical shapes in yellow, greens and blues. (Detail of* plate 1)

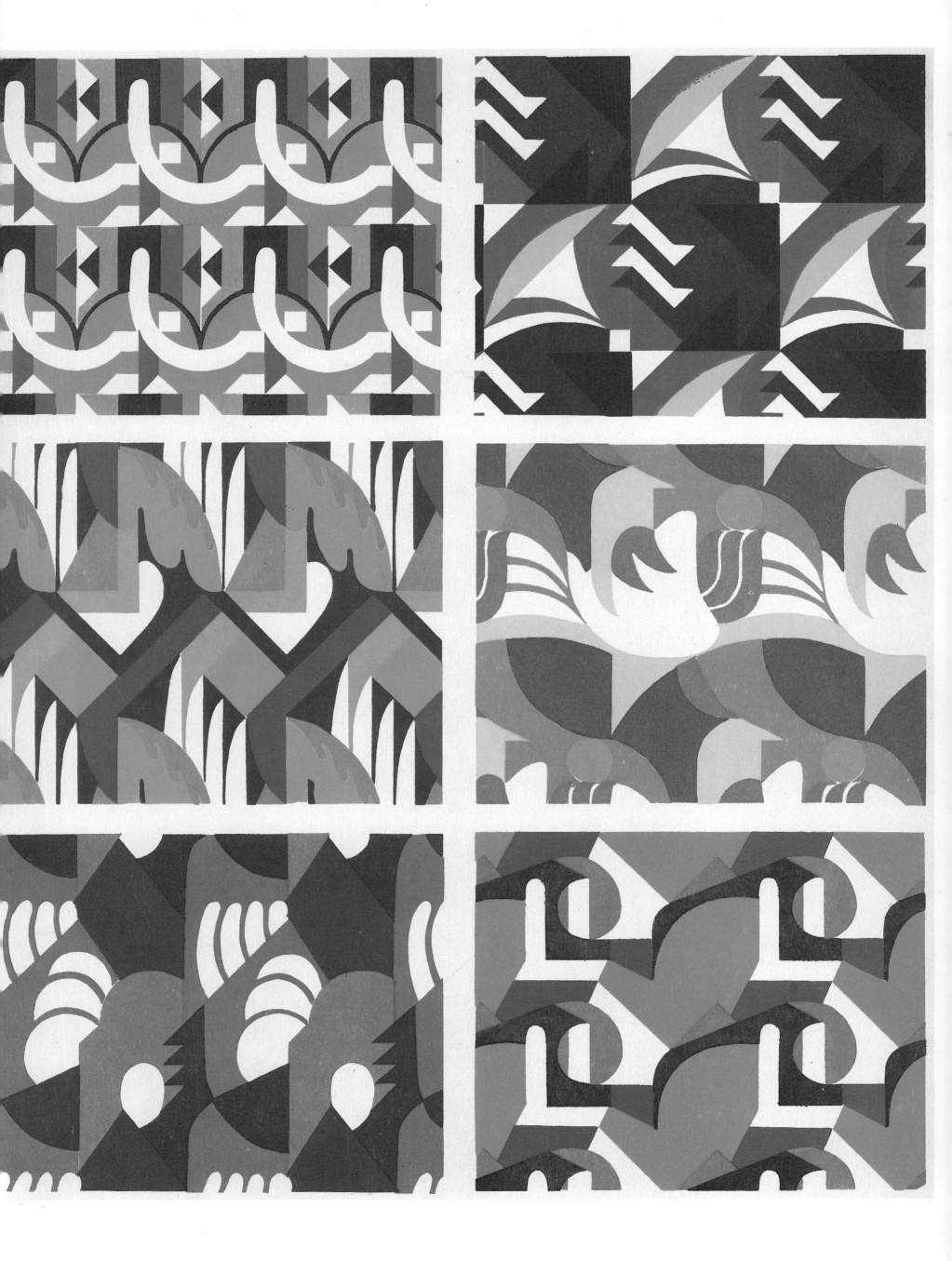

PLATE 4

Top right: *Pattern suggestive of a bird motif in which the neutral page colour is read as a positive shape*

PLATE 5

*Non-repeating design in predominantly secondary colours producing the effect of an evening landscape with full moons. (Detail of plate 4)*

PLATE 7

*Repeat pattern with spikes or fronds.*
(*Detail of* plate 6)

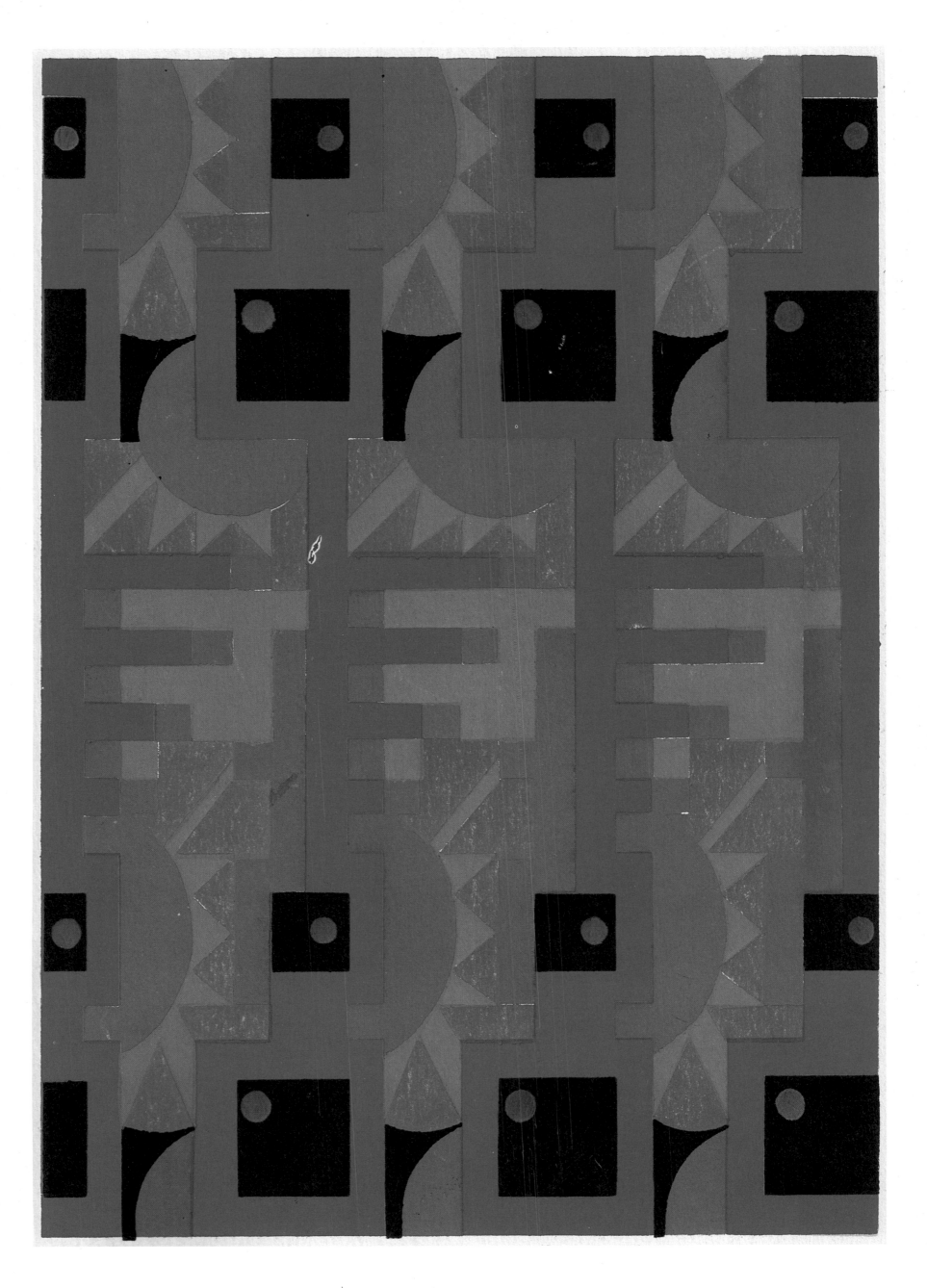

PLATE 8

*Repeat pattern with aggressive red/black contrast and mechanical 'cog' effect. (Detail of* plate 6)

PLATE 10
*Repeat pattern with stylized lighting effect.*
(*Detail of* plate 9)

PLATE 11

Top left: *Pattern of curved forms structured on a grid (compare with the organization of plate 10)*

Bottom left: *Repeat pattern which bears a superficial resemblance to the colour exercises of Josef Albers. Bright blue and muted green give an effect of overlap in black*

PLATE 13

Top left and top right: *Complementary borders in green and orange respectively. Each makes use of a hook or question mark shape*

Bottom: *Repeat pattern in earth tones and bright yellow. Forms resembling birds push outwards from a vertical axis*

PLATE 14

*Non-repeating asymmetrical design with sharp contrasts of tone emphasizing angularity and giving an illusion of three-dimensional space. (Detail of plate 13)*

PLATE 15

Top right: *Repeat pattern suggestive of figures in costume*

Bottom left: *Repeat pattern of cursive forms punctuated by purple dots*

Bottom right: *Simple geometric pattern of rectilinear shapes*

PLATE 16

*Geometric repeat pattern in muted primaries. (Detail of* plate 15)

PLATE 17

Top left: *Dense geometric pattern in which the contrasts of tone produce a hard-edged mechanical effect*

Bottom right: *Pattern developed from a square grid in which may be read a regular zig-zag running horizontally*

PLATE 19

Top right: *Non-repeating organic design with transparent and opaque overlaps producing a layered effect. Subject and background are clearly distinguishable despite their being no suggestion of representational form*

Bottom: *Anthropomorphic forms in a repeat which produces an effect of marching. (Compare with the structure of* plate 13 Bottom)

PLATE 21

Bottom left: *Grid pattern with limited tonal range*

Bottom right: *Repeat pattern with chequerboard effect and stripes*

PLATE 22

*Design in organic colours with repeated tree motif in silhouette. (Detail of* plate 21)

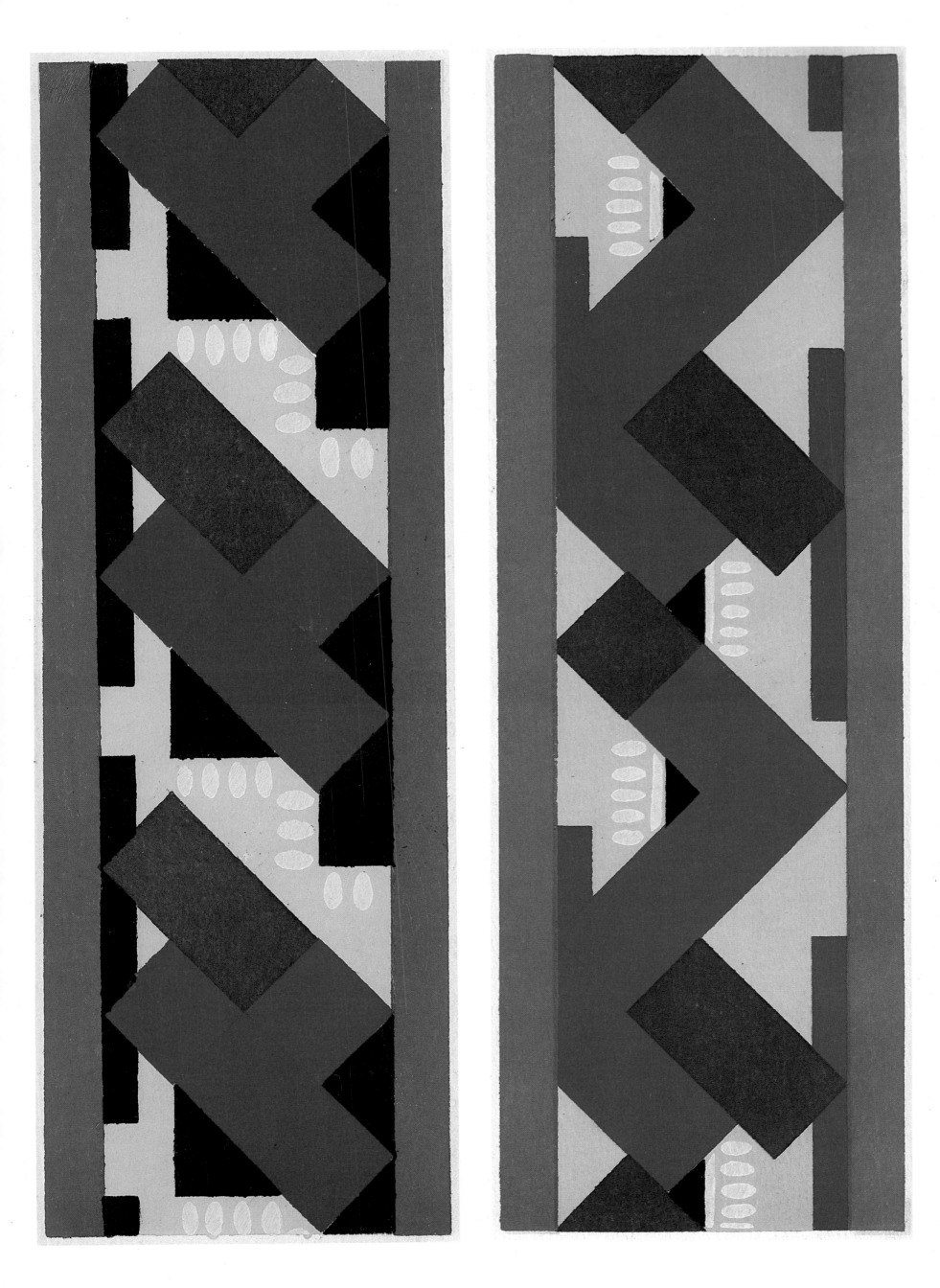

PLATE 27
*Detail of* plate 26

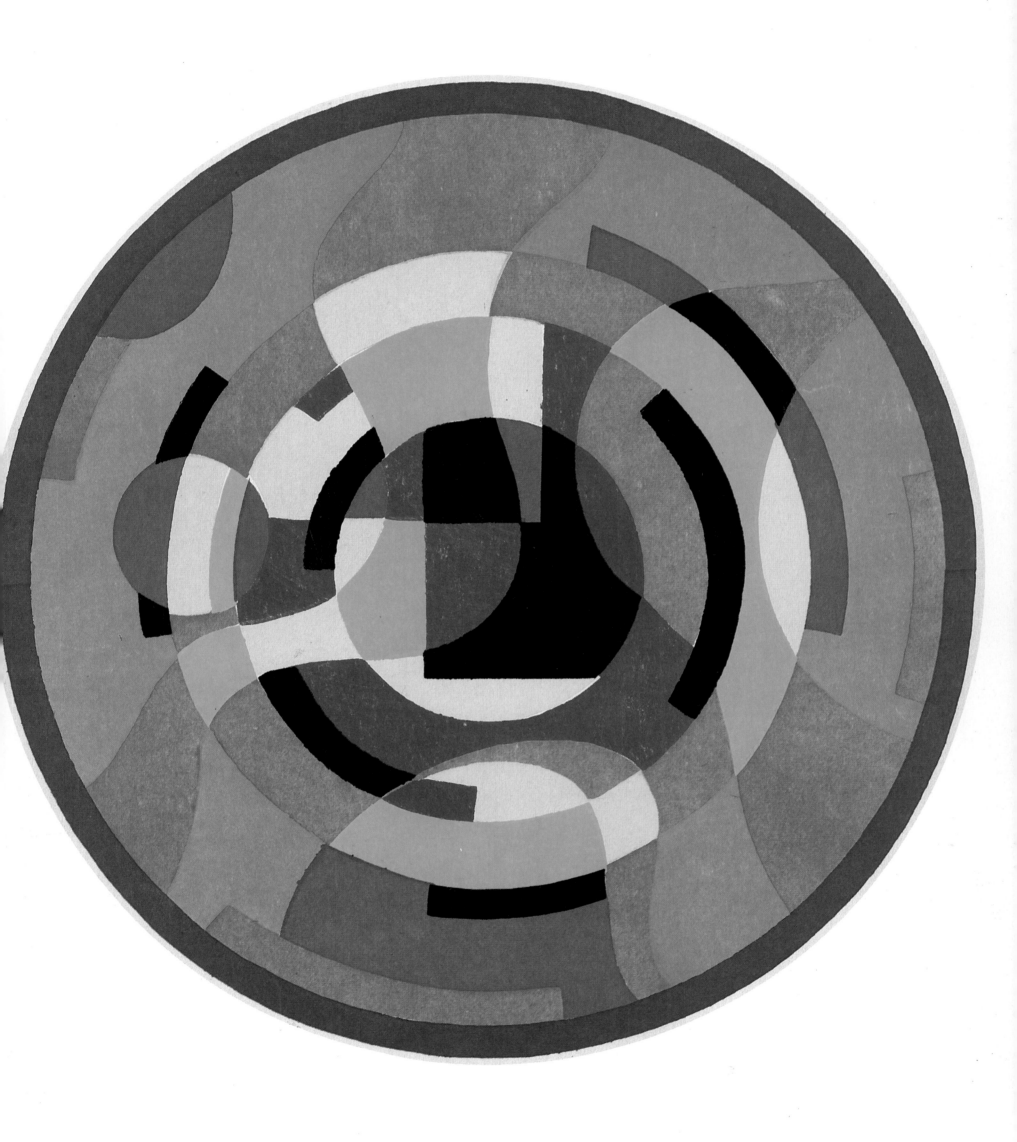

## PLATE 33

*Non-repeating design with transparent ray or shadow effect. (Detail of plate 32). This makes use of forms very similar to those in plate 32 Bottom right.*

PLATE 34

*Repeat pattern using strongly contrasting
colours and a variety of irregular shapes.
(Detail of* plate 32)

PLATE 35

Top left: *Design of protean shapes using predominantly secondary colours*

Top right: *Simple step pattern which creates a diagonal across a grid structure. The limited colour range produces an homogenous tonal effect*

Centre right: *Repeat pattern of opaque rectilinear forms in a muted colour range*

Bottom centre: *Grid pattern in natural hues with repeated abstract motif*

PLATE 36

Top right: *Discs resembling the Orphist colour circles of Robert Delaunay in a multicoloured pattern based on a grid (compare with the structure of* plate 1 Top centre, *the spacial arrangement of* plate 9 Bottom right, *and the form of* plate 31)

Bottom: *Sophisticated repeat pattern, possibly representative of a landscape with chequered sea and ball*

## PLATE 37

**Top left:** *Design with tubular effect creating strong sense of diagonal movement*

**Centre left:** *Almost monochrome pattern with repeat 'logo'*

**Bottom left:** *Repeat pattern on a vertical axis using forms strongly suggestive of punctuation or written symbols*

**Bottom right:** *Repeat pattern with lustrous effect created through gradations of tone*

PLATE 38

*Mechanistic or architectonic repeat pattern using a wide range of red/pink tones. (Detail of* plate 37)

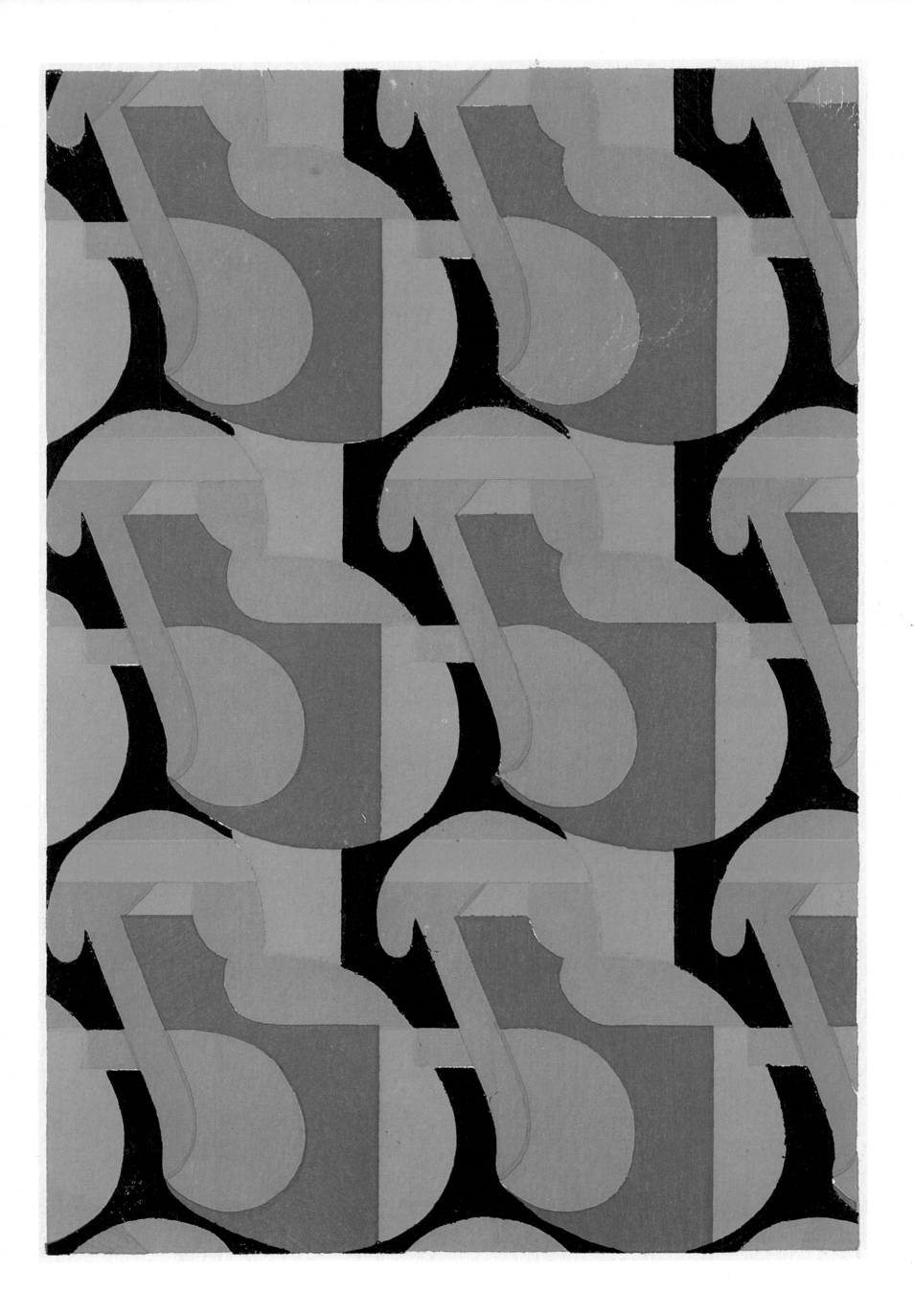

PLATE 40

*Simple repeat pattern of curves and right angles strongly suggestive of numeral or letter forms. (Detail of plate 39)*